W9-AXB-947

FOCUS ON DISASTERS

Flood

Fred Martin

RIGBY
INTERACTIVE LIBRARY

Designed by Raynor Design

Produced by Mandarin Offset Ltd.
Printed and bound in Hong Kong

99 98 97 96 95
10 9 8 7 6 5 4 3 2 1

ISBN 1-57572-020-5

Library of Congress Cataloguing in Publication Data

Martin, Fred. 1948–
    Flood/Fred Martin.
        p. cm.–(Focus on Disasters)
    Includes index.
    Summary: Examines how and why floods
    happen, their effects upon people and the
    environment, and what is being done to
    prevent future devastation.
    ISBN 1-57572-020-5 (lib.bdg.)
    1 Floods–Juvenile literature. [1. Floods.]
    I. Title. II. Series. Martin. Fred.
    1948– Focus on Disasters.
    GB1399.M7 1996
    363.3'493–dc20   95-38334

Acknowledgments
The Publishers would like to thank the following for permission to reproduce
photographs:
Richard Baker/Katz Pictures Ltd: p. 42; Bruce Coleman Ltd: pp. 5, 45; Comstock:
p. 38; Frank Lane Pictures: pp. 7, 8, 14, 30; Frank Spooner Picture Library: pp. 26, 27,
41; GeoScience Features: p. 36; Ben Gibson/Katz Pictures Ltd: p. 23; Glasgow Herald
and Evening Times: p. 18; Henry/REA/Katz Pictures Ltd: p. 19; Hutchison Library:
p. 17; J. Allan Cash Photo Library: pp. 9, 11, 21, 39; Brooks Kraft/Sygma: p. 25;
Oxford Scientific Films: p. 31; Panos Pictures: pp. 16, 20; Panos Pictures/Zed Nelson:
p. 29; C. Paris/REA/Katz Pictures Ltd: p. 4; Robert Harding Picture Library: pp.13,
32; Martin Sasse/Sygma: p. 12; Science Photo Library: pp. 15, 24, 40, 44; Still
Pictures: pp. 22, 43; Zefa UK Limited: p. 28.

All other photographs courtesy of the author.

Cover photograph © Frank Spooner Pictures/Christensen

Contents

Acts of God — 4

How Water Moves — 6

Where Rain Goes — 8

Rivers: Nature's Drains — 10

The Flood Risk — 12

River Flood Plains — 14

Living on Flood Plains — 16

Flooded Europe — 18

People Cause Floods — 20

Monsoon Floods — 22

The Mighty Mississippi — 24

The '93 Mississippi Floods — 26

Rivers Under Control — 28

Conserving Wetlands — 30

Eroding the Coast — 32

Tides and Weather — 34

Defending the Coast — 36

The Dutch Fight Back — 38

Saving Cities — 40

After the Flood — 42

Rising Seas — 44

Glossary — 46

Index — 48

Acts of God

EVERYBODY needs water. We need it to drink and to grow food. It is needed in factories to cool machinery and to help make goods. It also gives people great enjoyment when it flows as a river or when it washes up along a sandy coast. But we complain when there is too much water, and we have problems when there is too little. We have the most trouble when the power of water during a flood causes damage and sometimes deaths as well.

River Floods

Every river can flood. Most rivers do flood at least once every few years. The size of the river does not matter. Small mountain **streams** are just as likely to flood as the largest rivers. All that is needed is some flat land that the floodwater can flow over and cover. The water stays on the ground for a few hours to a few weeks before it drains back into the soil or river.

Some rivers have a yearly flood when the season changes from very dry to very wet. For others, the chances of a flood are not so easy to predict. No single reason may be enough to cause the flood. Instead, they flood when several things happen by chance at the same time.

Some of the worst and most unexpected floods have happened when snow begins to melt and there is very heavy rainfall at the same time. There is always a chance that this will happen, but it does not happen too often. Perhaps this is why floods are sometimes called an "act of God."

Photo Notes
- In 1993, rivers in Paris burst their banks and flooded parts of the town.
- Flood defenses were not able to control the floodwater.

Flooding by the Sea

Flooding by the sea happens where the land is low-lying and exposed to strong winds. Many of these places are where people have reclaimed land from the sea. This is land that naturally flooded every day for thousands of years before people drained and reclaimed it.

Some features along the coast, such as **beaches** and **sand dunes**, are natural defenses. These are made of sand and shingle that are carried there by the sea. They can also be carried away again to leave the land exposed to the force of wind and waves.

In the United States, many miles of coastline are defended by strong walls of stone and concrete. But sometimes the walls are not strong enough or high enough to survive everything that the sea can throw at them. The result is a flood that sweeps in over the land, causing great damage and sometimes deaths.

As with rivers, reasons for the worst sea floods are usually complex. The shape of the coastline, the time of high **tide** and the strength and direction of the wind can all play a part. The problems come when they act together by chance.

Photo Notes
- A Bible story tells about how a great flood covered the earth and how only Noah, his family, and two of every animal managed to survive.
- A rainbow is said to be a gift from God after the great flood.
- Some archeologists think that layers of fine mud beneath the ancient city of Ur show evidence for the great flood.

River and sea floods are part of the natural processes that shape our landscape. People also play a part in shaping the landscape by trying to stop these natural processes. Defenses against both rivers and the sea can work for a while. In the end however, it is an unequal battle that only the rivers and the sea can win.

DID YOU KNOW?

The worst flood disaster in the last 100 years was in 1931 when the Huang He River in China burst its banks. About one million people died in the flood. The Huang He is also called "China's sorrow" as it has a long history of flooding.

How Water Moves

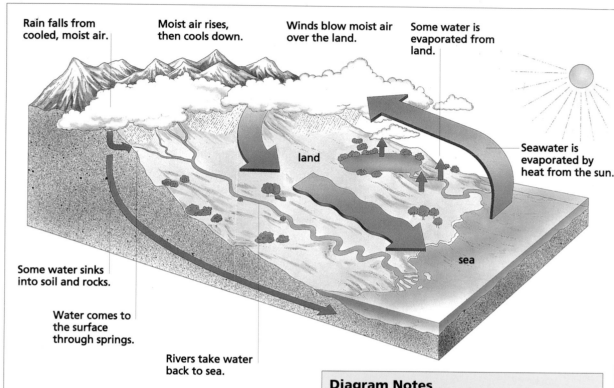

Rain falls from cooled, moist air.

Moist air rises, then cools down.

Winds blow moist air over the land.

Some water is evaporated from land.

Seawater is evaporated by heat from the sun.

land

Some water sinks into soil and rocks.

Water comes to the surface through springs.

Rivers take water back to sea.

sea

Diagram Notes
- Water is evaporated from seas and oceans.
- It rises into the air as a gas called water vapor.
- Cooling makes the water vapor condense back to droplets of water as clouds and then rain.
- Water flows back to the oceans in rivers to complete the water cycle.

WATER is a combination of one part hydrogen and two parts oxygen, (H_2O). Earth would be a dead and dry planet without it. Almost all of the earth's water is in seas and oceans. The rest is on the land in rivers and lakes, in rocks and soil, or in the air.

Water is always moving from place to place. It moves in ocean currents and it flows down rivers. Water is also in the air where it is blown by winds and falls as rain. Floods play a natural part in the way that water moves.

Liquid, Solid, and Gas

Water is a liquid when it is flowing in seas, lakes and rivers. If it freezes and changes to ice, it becomes a **solid**. Icebergs and glaciers store frozen water as a solid until they melt.

If the water is heated by the sun, it turns into a **gas** called **water vapor**. You cannot see this gas, but you may feel it in the air on a hot and humid day. Changing liquid water to water vapor is called **evaporation**.

Water vapor rises into the atmosphere and is blown by the wind. When it cools down it turns first to clouds and then sometimes to rain or snow. It is said to have **condensed** when it changes back from a gas to a liquid.

The Water Cycle

The sun gives the energy to evaporate and move water from the oceans to the land. The air's temperature changes as it moves from place to place. When air moves over warm land, it is warmed and starts to rise. As it gets higher, it cools and forms clouds and often rain. If air has to cross mountains, it is forced to rise. As it cools, clouds and rain can be expected over the mountains.

When rain reaches the ground, some of it evaporates back to the atmosphere. Some of the rest finds its way into rivers and so back to the sea. Water flows downhill so it keeps moving down to reach **sea level**.

If a river is short, rainwater can be back in the sea within a few days. If it falls as snow, it can stay on the ground for months or turn to ice and stay there for many years. In the end, it either melts or moves slowly to the sea in the form of glaciers or ice sheets. Water that sinks into rocks can stay there for thousands of years until it comes back to the surface.

Once water flows back to the sea, it starts the same circular route all over again. This route between sea, air, and land is called the **water cycle**.

A flood is just another part of the water cycle. It happens when too much water tries to get from one place to another place too quickly. When a river floods and spreads over the land, it is nature's way of storing the extra water for a short time. Flooding by the sea happens when water is pushed too hard against the coastline. Floods can cause human disasters, but they can also bring a few benefits.

Photo Notes
- A mountain stream in Norway.
- Snow that has fallen on the mountains has changed to ice.
- The ice has flowed down a valley as a glacier.
- The front of the glacier is melting, so the water can flow back to the sea again.

Where Rain Goes

RIVERS flood when they have to take too much water in a short time. The amount of water in a river depends on how rainwater gets there. A small amount of rain falls directly into rivers and onto lakes. But by far the greatest amount falls on the ground. From there, some of it finds its way to the rivers. It does this in a great variety of ways and over very different lengths of time.

Falling On Trees

A large amount of rainwater does not reach the rivers at all. On a warm day, the sun, helped by a gentle breeze, evaporates rainwater before it has a chance to go anywhere. This is what happens to wet clothes hung on a clothesline.

The amount and type of vegetation also affects how much water evaporates. In a tropical rain forest, the tree tops are so close together that very little rain can get through to the ground.

There is usually a daily downpour in these areas. Water that stays on the branches and leaves evaporates quickly. It rises, forming more clouds, and then comes back down as a rainstorm the next day.

Some water from trees does drip onto the ground then into the soil. Much of this is taken back up into the trees through their roots. It reaches the leaves where it is passed back to the air by **transpiration**.

When there is a large amount of evaporation and transpiration, most of the rain does not get as far as the rivers. This means there is little chance of a flood. This could be a lesson for people who want to cut down too many trees.

> **Photo Notes**
> - The tropical rain forest in Costa Rica.
> - Rainwater is evaporating from the leaves after a daily rainstorm.
> - Some rain drips to the ground but is taken back up into the trees.
> - Only a small amount of what has fallen is left to flow to the rivers.

Rain Reaches the Rivers

Rainwater that falls on bare soil or rock can sink underground. This is called **infiltration**. It sinks down through small spaces called **pores** in the soil or rock. Cracks in the rock also let water sink down into them. A rock that lets a large amount of water sink into it is called a **permeable** rock. Limestone and sandstone are very permeable rocks, so they soak up a large amount of rainwater. In some types of limestone, the water disappears underground into caves.

Water sinks until it reaches a saturated layer where all the pore spaces and cracks are already filled with water. The level at the top of this saturated layer is called the **water table**. If the water table comes up to the earth's surface, a river can start to flow from a **spring**.

Some rainwater flows directly over the surface into rivers. This is called **surface run-off**. There is usually most surface run-off when the ground is **impermeable**. This means that water cannot sink into it. Hard rocks such as granite do not have pore spaces or wide cracks, so not much rain can sink down into it. Clay is also impermeable. That is why it turns to mud when it rains.

Surface run-off is the fastest way that most water gets into a river. If most of the water usually does this, the river **channel** may be big enough to take the run-off without causing a flood. If a large amount of surface run-off only happens from time to time, the channel may not be able to take the sudden extra amount flowing into it. This is when a flood can be expected.

On flat ground where the rock is impermeable, water cannot sink down or flow away. Instead, it lies there making a marsh. Permeable rocks and marshes act as giant sponges that soak up rain, then slowly release it again long after the rain has stopped.

DID YOU KNOW?

Almost three-quarters of all the rain and snow that falls in the United States evaporates. Just over one-quarter flows back to the oceans in rivers.

Rivers: Nature's Drains

RIVERS are nature's drains. They take water from the land back to the sea. Small streams flow into larger ones, which then join to make rivers. Floods are part of the way an area is drained. They happen when the streams and rivers are not big enough to take what goes into them.

Drainage Basins

An area drained by a river is called a **drainage basin**. Rain that does not evaporate is taken back to the sea by the rivers that flow through the drainage basin. The boundary line around the drainage basin is called a **watershed**. Rain falling on different sides of the watershed goes into different drainage basins.

Water in a drainage basin begins to flow in streams. Some rivers start from a melting glacier, a lake, a spring, or an area of upland marsh. These places are called the river's **source**. The Rhône River in France starts from a melting glacier in the Alps. The Mississippi River starts from a spring 10 feet wide and 3 feet deep.

Other rivers begin as sheets of water that flow down a steep slope. The water cuts small channels that become deeper when they join others. Soon the main channel becomes a stream with many smaller channels feeding water into it.

Photo Notes

- Mountain streams start.
- Two streams have cut deep gulleys into the slope that leads up to the watershed ridge of this small part of a drainage basin.
- The two streams flow for a short distance, then join each other to make a larger stream.
- Water flows quickly down the slopes into these streams.

The Drainage System

A river is formed as streams join together. Each stream takes water from its own small drainage basin. A river that joins a larger river is called a **tributary**. More rivers from other drainage basins keep joining until there is a whole network of streams and rivers flowing into one main river. The whole network of streams and rivers is called a **river system**.

The drainage basin of the Amazon river and its tributaries is about 2 million square miles, or over half the size of the United States. All rainfall in the Amazon's drainage basin either evaporates or flows to the Atlantic Ocean. The flow varies from 8 to 30 million gallons every second, about 20 percent of all the water from all the world's rivers.

A river flows out to the sea at its **mouth**. Rivers such as the Severn in England have a long **estuary** where the mouth slowly widens to meet the sea. The Severn estuary widens to 2 miles, but the mouth of the Amazon is about 150 miles wide.

Too much rain in only part of a drainage basin can cause a flood and surprise people living downstream where it may not have rained at all. When the rain stops and the river level falls again, the floodwater either sinks into the ground or drains back into the channel. The river system has done its job, though for a while, it may cause problems for people who live near it.

Photo Notes
- The Niger River is joined by the Benue River about 280 miles from where it enters the sea in the Gulf of Guinea.
- The Niger starts to flow in Guinea, which is 125 miles to the west.
- The Benue starts in Cameroon about 500 miles to the east.

The Flood Risk

RIVERS and streams can change from gentle flows to raging torrents. At one time of the year, the water may dry up completely. A few months later, there can be a raging torrent that bursts its banks. Some rivers change in this way every year, so their floods can be expected. Floods that come without enough warning are the ones that cause the greatest problems.

Rainfall and River Flow

The amount of water flowing in a river is called its **discharge**. The change in a river's discharge from month to month is called the river's **regime**. In the United States, there is usually enough rain every month to keep the rivers flowing. Their discharge does change, but only the smallest streams ever dry up. An exceptional amount of rain is needed for the rivers to flood.

In other countries, the climate can be very different. In India's **monsoon** climate, there is a dry season with very little rain for six months. This is followed by very heavy rain for the next few months. Rivers swell and can flood during the rains, then dry up completely when the rains stop.

Rivers that flow from high mountains can change their discharge very quickly and unexpectedly. For months, little water gets down to the rivers. It stays locked up as snow and ice.

A sudden rise in the temperature can change all that. The ice starts to melt and millions of gallons of water are released. If there is more rain at the same time, the result is likely to be a flood.

The Rhine River flows from the Alps through Switzerland, Germany, and then the Netherlands. Floods from melting snow and glacier ice have always made it dangerous for people who live near the river banks. In spite of work that has been done to stop flooding, the river still causes problems.

Photo Notes
- The Rhine River burst its banks in the winter of 1993.
- Low-lying parts of cities along the river were flooded.
- The river channel was not able to cope with rainfall that was well above average.

Flash Floods

In desert areas, there may be no rain for months or even years. The surface is likely to be bare rock, stones, or baked mud, and there is little vegetation. When it does rain, the rainfall is sudden, short, and very heavy. Almost all the water then flows as surface run-off. It quickly flows into old dried up channels. Soon the channels overflow as a **flash flood**. In June 1993, 21 people were killed when a flash flood swept through Shadyside in Ohio. There is seldom any warning that a flash flood will strike.

In wetter areas, the month of August is when flash floods are most common. If the summer is dry, the ground is baked hard by the sun. Conditions are just right for a flash flood.

As the day's heat builds up, air starts to rise over the land. Water vapor blown in from the sea and from evaporation over land forms giant thunder clouds. These are called **cumulonimbus** clouds. The rising temperature keeps the water vapor in the air. Raindrops grow until they suddenly fall in a **cloudburst**.

One place can be affected by a cloudburst, but another only a few miles away may have no rain at all. This makes it impossible to give warning that any one river is going to be affected. Anyone enjoying a quiet day's fishing or a walk along a river bank will need to move quickly to avoid being swept away. A person can be swept away in fast-flowing water that is only up to the knees.

DID YOU KNOW?

In January 1994, the small Lavant River, through Chichester in Great Britain, burst its banks and flooded a large part of the town. By August, the riverbed through the town was completely dry.

River Flood Plains

Photo Notes
- The Dee River and its valley in north Wales.
- The river is meandering from side to side.
- The meanders move downstream by eroding on one side of the meander bend and depositing on the other side.
- Meandering has made a wide, flat flood plain.

RIVERS carve out the valleys they flow in. They do this by slowly wearing away their beds and by wearing away their banks. This makes the valley both lower and wider. Floods also play a part in giving a valley its natural shape.

A River Flood Plain

Rivers carry their water in a river channel. Seen from above, the channels snake from side to side in bends that are called **meanders**. In a meander bend, fast-flowing water wears away soil and rock on the outside of the bend. Erosion is said to be taking place. These pieces of soil and rock are carried along until the river drops them again. The larger pieces are dropped where the river slows down on the inside of the next meander bend. This is where there is **deposition**.

A meander is never in the same place for long. It moves downstream as if the river was held at its source and shaken like a rope. The meanders work their way over the whole valley bottom making it both flatter and wider. This is the ground that is flooded if the river bursts its banks or flows over them. This flat land is called the valley **flood plain**.

River Mud

When a river floods, water flows out over the flood plain and settles there for a while. Soil and other small pieces of rock it is carrying are dropped on the flood plain. This material is called **alluvium**. Fine mud that is dropped is called **silt**.

Some water sinks down into the soil unless the ground is already saturated. Most of it flows back into the river channel as the water level goes down again. As it drains back, more pieces are dropped at the top of the bank. This builds up to form natural embankments called **levees**.

Rivers sometimes flow between high levees and above their own flood plains on thick layers of alluvium that they have dropped. People often build the levees even higher to stop the rivers from flooding. If a levee is broken, the river pours onto the valley land below. The only way to get the water back into the river is to repair the levee and then pump the water back.

The smallest pieces of river mud are carried all the way to the river's mouth before they are finally dropped. As the river enters the sea, it slows down and drops its load of silt. A delta is formed if currents along the coast do not take the silt away. The Mississippi Delta is one of the largest. Vegetation takes root in the rich mud and turns some parts of the delta into dry land. The rest is left as winding creeks called bayous.

Some of the world's great natural **wetlands**, such as the bayous at the mouth of the Mississippi River are in deltas.

Photo Notes
- The Severn River in flood.
- Rich alluvial soils make good farmland for grazing animals.
- An electricity power station uses river water to cool steam back to water.

Living on Flood Plains

People have always lived near rivers. The first civilizations grew up in river valleys in Egypt, India, and the Middle East.

There is always the risk of flooding, but there are some very good reasons why people have been prepared to take the risk.

Cities by Rivers

Villages, towns, and cities have grown beside rivers. The most basic reason for this is that people need water to drink. In some places, rivers are still used for this reason. Towns grew where a large river could be crossed at a shallow point called a ford. The city of Oxford in England is one example of where this happened. In time, the ford was replaced by a bridge. Roads met at bridges, so these were good places for farmers and traders to buy and sell goods.

A river bend also made it easier to defend a town, because it acts as a natural moat.

Rivers are used to power and to cool machinery and to produce goods that need large amounts of water, such as wool. River valleys make easy routes for roads, railroads, and canals. Roads often run along the valley sides just above the valley bottom to avoid being flooded. Embankments raise railroad lines above the flood levels.

At first, places that might flood were avoided. This changed as better ways were found to protect and drain the land.

Photo Notes
- The city of Dhaka in Bangladesh under floodwater in 1988.
- The city is built on flat land in the delta area of the Ganges and Brahmaputra rivers.
- The city has been flooded many times with great loss of life and damage to property.

Now there are houses, factories, and other buildings on flood plains. Sometimes people forget about the risk of floods, and the river proves to be too powerful.

Using Flood Plains

Valley bottoms are good places for some types of farming. The land is flat, and the **alluvial** soil is deep and fertile. Grass for grazing grows well in damp conditions, and if there is a flood, animals can be quickly moved away.

People in some Asian countries have a difficult choice to make. They can grow food on land that floods and risk having their homes flooded as well. Or they can live more safely on land where food is harder to grow. Often there is no choice at all. People carry on living where they can find work or where their land is.

Fine mud is only one material that is washed down in rivers. They also carry and drop larger pieces of sand and gravel. These are quarried and used for building. Gravel is mixed with concrete and used to build roads. A hole is left in the ground when the sand and gravel have been removed. These soon fill up with water to become small lakes. They are often used for boating and other types of recreation. Some are used as nature reserves. This is a good idea, because it helps to replace the natural wetland areas that have been lost when land is drained for farming and building.

DID YOU KNOW?

The valleys in India, China, and other countries in Asia are used for growing rice and other crops. Water from the rivers is used to irrigate the crops. People also depend on the floods to bring new soil, called silt, to the fields every year. Crops do not grow as well without the new soil. Without it, expensive fertilizers would have to be used. These can be too expensive for poor farmers to buy.

Flooded Europe

Floods leave a trail of destruction wherever they strike. Flood defenses never seem to be enough to protect everyone, even in countries where there is enough wealth to build them. Rivers cannot be put behind concrete walls from source to mouth. In 1993, news reports of floods from countries all over Europe told the same kind of story. The reasons for the floods were not unusual, but their number and the amount of destruction they caused took most people by surprise.

Winter Floods

In Scotland, the year started badly for people on a housing estate in Perth. The Tay River burst its banks. There was a warning that this might happen, and a "red alert" was issued. In only 30 minutes, a large part of the estate was under water. Few people wanted to leave their homes, so they found themselves trapped.

When the floodwater went down, there were dirty water marks and mud in all the houses. Carpets, furniture, and other belongings had been ruined. Not everyone was insured against flood, so they were left to pay for the damage.

The cause of the flood began in the Grampian Mountains where the Tay has its source. It had been a very cold December and there was 5 feet of snow lying on the ground. Soil was frozen so nothing could sink through it. Then the temperature suddenly started to rise. At first, it rose by 7° F, then by another 18° F. The snow and ice quickly started to melt.

At the same time, it started to rain heavily. About 4 inches of rain fell in a few days. Within a few days, the Tay was carrying eight times more water than normal. This burst the banks and caused the flooding.

Summer Floods

The late spring, summer, and early autumn brought some of the wettest weather in recent years to many parts of Europe. In Devon in southwest England, swollen rivers rushed down from the uplands and flooded the coastal towns.

Photo Notes
- Flooding from the Tay River in Perth in the winter of 1993.
- Melting snow and heavy rain combined to make the river burst its banks.
- A flood warning was given, but most people stayed in their homes and had to be rescued.

In the seaside resort of Llandudno in north Wales, 1,000 people had to leave their homes because of flooding. In Berkshire, 2 inches of rain fell in three hours, as much as normally falls in a month. An expressway had to be closed because there was so much water on its surface.

The thunderstorms causing the floods had come to Britain in weather systems that brought warm, moist air over the country. Heat from the ground made the air rise and form giant rain clouds. Storm clouds are watched on weather radar, but it is hard to predict exactly where or when the rain will fall.

By September, southern Europe was also being affected by thunderstorms. In Spain, 2 inches of rain fell in one day. The average for the month is less than half an inch. Six people were killed in northern Italy as heavy rain and gales caused flash floods. One town in Switzerland was covered by 10 feet of floodwater. In October, Venice was flooded and lakes overflowed.

The downpours were the immediate cause of the floods, but the problem was made worse by the fact that rainfall earlier in the year had also been above average and the ground was **waterlogged**. Rain from the thunderstorms was not able to sink into the waterlogged ground, so it ran straight into the rivers. It is often the case that the worst problems are caused when two or more things happen at the same time.

DID YOU KNOW?

The National Weather Service River Forecast Center issues flood forecasts. "Flood warning" means danger is slow to come. "Flash-flood watch" means danger is near.

People Cause Floods

RIVERS flood when too much water tries to get into them too quickly. The time taken for water to get into streams and rivers depends partly on the amount of rain that falls and partly on where it goes when it reaches the ground. People use the land in many different ways. Some uses of land increase the risk of floods.

How Land is Used

Less rainwater gets to a river from a forest than from an area of bare plowed fields. There is more evaporation and less run-off from a forest. It also takes much longer for the water to get into the soil or to flow as run-off.

If trees are cut down, the flow of water in nearby rivers is increased as rain flows off bare land. Soil is washed away by the force of the rain. It clogs up the river channel making less room for water. This also increases the flood risk.

One of the greatest changes taking place to the earth's environment at the moment is that trees are being cut down. This is called **deforestation**. People have always cut down trees. Now the problem is mainly in the tropical rain forests in Africa, South America, and Southeast Asia. People are desperate to have more land for farming and to make money by selling the wood. Replanting and conservation are not easy in places where the population is increasing and there is so much poverty.

There is very little natural forest left in the Himalayan Mountains. Trees have been cut down to give people more land to farm. Even the steepest slopes have been cut bare.

Photo Notes
- Steep hillside in the Himalayan Mountains in Nepal in Asia.
- Farmers have cut down trees to get more land to farm.
- Rain is washing soil off the land and into the rivers.
- Deep gulleys are cut in the hillsides by the rainwater.
- Water gets quickly into the rivers and causes flooding.

Rain now washes quickly down the slopes and into the rivers. Soil is washed down the slopes as well. The result seems to be an increase in the number of floods that affect both the mountains and the lowland areas downstream.

Draining the Land

There is a greater risk of floods when houses, factories, and roads are built. Rivers that flow through these areas need to be **managed** so that they do not flood. Flood defenses can be built to make sure that people are kept safe. Banks are made higher and stronger so that the water stays in its channel. This solves the problem in one place, but the water then flows further downstream until it can overflow the banks and flood somewhere and someone else.

There is less countryside now than in the past. Towns and cities have become larger while forests have become smaller. Building changes the type of ground that rainwater falls on. Instead of falling on trees or soaking into the soil, it falls on concrete and other hard surfaces. Water cannot sink into concrete and tarmac, so drains have to be built. Flat sports fields also have to be properly drained.

Water is dangerous to drivers if it is left on the roads. Drains are designed to take water off the surface quickly and get it to streams and rivers. During a rainstorm, water flows quickly into the drains then straight to rivers through pipes. This reduces the time that it takes for water to get into the rivers. This can increase the chance of flooding.

Drains can also be put into land that farmers want to use. Crops can go rotten if they are left in waterlogged soil for too long. The farmer gets better drainage by making sure that water quickly flows away to the rivers.

It seems that the best way to reduce the risk of flooding is to make sure that land is used in ways that do not add to the problem. Any changes to how land is used need to take into account how the rivers might be affected. It makes more sense not to cause the problem in the first place than to try to stop it once it starts.

Photo Notes
- A building site where drains are being put in to get water off the ground.
- Water will flow quickly into the drains during a rainstorm, then it will flow into the rivers.

Monsoon Floods

THERE are more deaths from floods in the monsoon countries of Asia every year than in any other part of the world. About 500 people died in one recent flood in India. Unfortunately this number of deaths is not unusual. The monsoon climate causes heavy rain and floods. There is often not enough money either to control the rivers or to help people when a flood does happen.

Monsoon Rains

A monsoon climate divides the year in two. Six months are warm and very dry as winds blow off the land. Then the wind changes direction and blows in from the sea. This brings hot, and very wet air over the land. This hot, wet air is what causes the heavy rains to fall. It is not unusual for more rain to fall in just the three wettest months in India or the Philippines than falls all year in most parts of the United States.

Some of the largest rivers have their source in the Himalayan Mountains. The Ganges, Indus, and Brahmaputra are three. Rain that falls on the mountains runs quickly into the streams that feed these rivers. In recent years, the amount of surface run-off has increased because so many trees have been cut down. This also causes landslides, which collapse into the rivers and cause floods.

Photo Notes

- A flash flood in the Philippines has wrecked this area of shantytown houses.
- Logs and other debris in the water makes the damage worse.
- Many people blame the floods on changes to the natural vegetation in the drainage basins of these streams.
- Trees have been cut down for timber and to grow crops.

Photo Notes
- Bangladesh floods in 1988.
- The village has been completely cut off by floodwater.
- Crops have been flooded and ruined.
- After the floods, the survivors move back and start all over again.

Rivers in the Philippines are much shorter than those in India, but monsoon rains also make them swell and burst their banks. Flash floods come quickly and with great force. Poor people have to build houses illegally on land that is not safe. Houses built from wood and scrap materials are easily washed away. The number of flood disasters has been increasing as more trees have been cut down for timber and to grow crops.

Disasters in Bangladesh

Bangladesh is a small country and one of the world's poorest. It has also had more than its share of natural disasters. About 110 million people live there. Eight out of every ten live in countryside areas where they depend on farming to make a living. Most live in the flat delta land where the Ganges and Brahmaputra rivers flow out to the sea. There is nowhere to go when the rivers or the sea start to flood. The people cope well with normal floods, but heavy floods cause terrible hardship.

By the time the Ganges and Brahmaputra rivers reach Bangladesh, they have both flowed for more than 1,550 miles. Every one of their tributaries has also joined them bringing rainwater from both of their drainage basins. Flood defenses have been built in Bangladesh and are being improved, but the problem is just too great and there is too little money available to solve it.

Floods from the sea come when typhoons move up over the Bay of Bengal, a part of the Indian Ocean, and hit the delta area. The sea and rivers combine to bring one disaster after another. Homes are washed away, crops are ruined, and saltwater gets into the soil.

The floods have increased and have become more devastating. In September 1986, 42 people died and 100,000 were made homeless during one flood. A year later, 1,240 more people died in floods and three million tons of crops were ruined. In 1988, thousands more were killed and 25 million people were made homeless. This time, it was a typhoon and sea flooding that did the damage. The death toll has continued into the 1990s, and it looks as if it will go on in the future.

More people will be affected as the population of Bangladesh increases. People move onto unprotected delta land, because there is a shortage of farmland. This exposes them to even more risks. For the moment, they seem to have no other choice.

DID YOU KNOW?

Bangladesh is one of the most crowded countries in the world. There are about 800 people for every square mile. This is a very high figure when so many people live in the countryside.

The Mighty Mississippi

SOME rivers are record breakers. They are longer, wider, or drain a larger area than all the others. When they flood, the damage they cause can also break records. In 1993, the Mississippi flooded in a way that was not expected. Flood defenses that had been built after previous floods proved to be too low and not strong enough. It seems that the more the river is contained, the worse the floods are when they happen.

Mississippi Profile

The Mississippi River is one of the world's great rivers. It flows for 2,330 miles from its source in northern Minnesota to its mouth near New Orleans. About two-thirds of the United States is drained by the Mississippi and the tributaries that flow into it. Some of these tributaries are major rivers themselves, such as the Missouri, the Tennessee, and the Ohio rivers.

At New Orleans, the river is almost half a mile wide, though it is more than a mile wide further upstream. By the time it enters the sea, it is carrying about 150 cubic miles of water each year. It also dumps 11 billion cubic feet of mud into the delta area and the Gulf of Mexico.

The shape of the valley has been made by the river and its floods over millions of years. It has meandered over the valley floor, making it wider and flatter. In some places, it is almost 75 miles wide. It is easy to see old meanders on a satellite image of the area. Some of these have formed where the river has naturally broken through a meander.

Photo Notes

- A satellite image showing the Mississippi and Missouri rivers in 1988.
- The city of St. Louis is shown at the bottom of the picture.
- The rectangles of pink, yellow, and green show the valley bottom.
- Most of the valley bottom was flooded by July 1989.

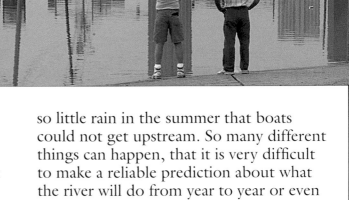

Others are where people have changed the river's course by digging out a new channel. The valley soil is made from the rich alluvium that the river has washed down and dumped during floods. Even now, the river is trying to do what it has always done, but people are trying to stop it.

Managing the Mississippi

Like all great rivers, the Mississippi has attracted people to live on its banks and wide, flat valley bottom. Cities such as Memphis and St. Louis have become important centers for industry and trade. Farmers use the land to grow all kinds of crops, from cotton in the south to wheat in the north. The river is used by ships and barges for much of its course. A river that can be used by boats is said to be **navigable**.

A river this size and with so many people depending on it has to be managed. Levees have been built to make sure the river does not flood. Meander bends have been cut off to make the river flow faster, so that alluvium is washed away and the river bed does not become clogged with mud. A straighter river also means that the boats that use it have a shorter distance to travel.

The river's flow changes from month to month depending on the weather in different parts of its vast drainage basin. Spring and early summer bring melted snow from the mountains. Summer rains are unreliable, but can swell the river when they come. In one recent year, there was so little rain in the summer that boats could not get upstream. So many different things can happen, that it is very difficult to make a reliable prediction about what the river will do from year to year or even month to month.

The Mississippi has a long history of floods in spite of all the attempts to control it. There is a major flood about once every 10 years. Each time this happens, the people have to dry out their homes, rebuild what has been damaged, and count the cost in human lives.

Every year, there are more people living in the Mississippi Valley. The value of homes, farms, and businesses also increases. This increases the amount of damage that can be caused by floods. The flood of 1993 was one of the worst on record. The cost of the damage was also a record. In 1995, the Mississippi flooded again. Many people living in the flood plain, realizing that their homes and possessions would always be in danger, decided to leave the area permanently.

DID YOU KNOW?

In 1883, the writer Mark Twain wrote, "You cannot contain that lawless stream." He was writing about the Mississippi.

The '93 Mississippi Floods

BY the early summer of 1993, people in the Mississippi Valley were looking forward to their usual long and dry summer. The months before had been unusually wet, and everyone was waiting for the change. The last thing they wanted or expected was what happened next.

Rain and More Rain

The previous months had been wetter than average and in places, the ground was completely waterlogged. Then instead of becoming drier, more rain continued to fall. Cold, dry air from the north moved south and met warm, moist air that was moving north. This forced the warm air to rise and form dense clouds. Then it rained and kept on raining. It rained every day for 49 days. The extra rainwater flowed off the waterlogged land and filled the rivers until they flooded.

The floods began in Minnesota in the north of the drainage basin. The river first broke its banks in June. By July, the flooding had moved south into Illinois, Ohio, and seven other states. All along the river, water flowed through or over the levees. By early August, there was flooding as far south as Tennessee and Arkansas. Lands in nine Midwest states were declared "disaster areas." The whole state of Iowa was a disaster area. Once the water was over the levees, there was nothing to stop it from flowing over the flat valley bottom.

Photo Notes

- Sandbags have been piled up to try to stop the river from overflowing.
- Water is being pumped back into the river.

Flood Damage

People tried to stop the floods by using sandbags to build up the levees. Neighbors and the National Guard all worked to make the levees higher and to protect their homes, but nothing seemed to work. Some of the sandbags were sent from Bangladesh.

The river kept on rising. Farms were cut off and roads became impassable. River water 10 feet deep flowed for more than 5 miles over the valley bottom. St. Louis had river defenses high enough to contain a 50-foot rise in the river level. The river rose to 49.6 feet. Towns and farmland downstream were flooded.

When the floodwaters went down, 50 people had been killed, thousands of homes had been flooded, and some homes had been destroyed. Farm animals had also died, and crops of wheat, soybeans, and corn were ruined. Roads were washed away, and there were great gaps in the levees. The cost of the damage was about $10 billion.

There is no way of knowing when a flood like this will happen again. Some say it will happen once every 100 years. But in fact, the Mississippi flooded again in 1995. In some places the damage was worse than in 1993. The people have a difficult decision to make. They can spend money repairing the damage to property and rebuilding the levees higher and stronger. The problem will then be worse for places downstream that are not protected. It would be too expensive to protect the whole of the Mississippi as well as its tributaries.

Another answer is to let the river flood in some places that could be special wetland areas. It would mean that some people would have to move out and start their lives again somewhere else. Some land could be used in other ways so that it would not matter if it did flood. Either building better defenses or making land suitable for flooding is bound to cost a lot of money. Something must be done, and people must not forget what the Mississippi can do.

DID YOU KNOW? [?]

The loss of so much food from the Mississippi Valley meant that farmers in other places were able to raise their prices. It seems that some people are able to benefit from even the worst disasters.

Rivers Under Control

RIVERS need to be brought under some kind of control so that they can be used for transport and people can live near them safely. There are many ways this can be done.

Controlling the Flow

Locks and weirs control a river's speed by breaking up the river's natural drop. The river flows evenly between each weir. Boats are let down or brought up through the lock.

Navigation can be made easier by making a river channel deeper. This is done by dredging out sand and mud. One problem is that this can also cause the river to flow faster.

Barriers across a river can also slow down its flow and help hold back some water. These can be raised or lowered depending on the amount of water in the river.

Large dams and **reservoirs** stop rivers from flowing naturally. These are built for many reasons. They give a reliable source of drinking water and water to irrigate farmland, and they can be used to generate electricity. The reservoir stores water from wetter months until it is needed in the drier months. Storing water in this way helps to even out the river's flow throughout the year.

Photo Notes
- The Roosevelt Dam on the Salt River in Arizona.
- The river's natural flow is held back by the dam, which has formed a reservoir behind it.
- Water is used to generate electricity.

Photo Notes
- Embankments to keep a river in its channel in Bangladesh.
- Rock and soil have been heaped up to stop floodwater from spreading out over the flat landscape.

River Bank Management

Rivers wear away their banks as they meander from side to side. They take a long time to do this, but changes can happen suddenly. During a flood, the river flows both fast and deep. This is when the banks are at greatest risk of being scoured away and broken.

The point of greatest risk is on the outside of a river bend. This is where river banks need to be protected most. Sheets of concrete or steel piles can do this for a time. Wire cages filled with stones are also used. These are called **gabions**. The river bank is made stronger in one place, but there is still a problem. The bank can still be worn away in places just before or just after the reinforcements. The defenses are also made useless if water gets around behind them.

More water can be kept in a river channel if the banks are built higher. This is done by building levees. Piles of earth and rock are heaped up along the top of both river banks. Stronger materials such as rock and concrete will last longer.

In China, people have been raising the height of the levees on the Huang He for hundreds of years. The work has been done by hand rather than by machinery. Everyone in a village comes to do the work, because everyone is at risk.

Nature has its own way of protecting river banks. Thick clumps of reeds and rushes break up the river's flow along the sides. This is an effective and attractive way to protect a river bank.

DID YOU KNOW?

Barge owners on the Mississippi say that over the last 20 years they have needed much larger engines on their boats to get upstream. They blame the dredging that has been done to stop the river from flooding, which has made the river flow faster.

Conserving Wetlands

LAND that floods is not usually much use to farmers or anyone else. This is why so many areas that used to flood have now been drained and are protected from flooding in the future. This is true for flooding by both rivers and the sea. The work of **land reclamation** has turned floodland into dry land to be used for farming, industry, and homes.

Wetland Habitats

So many wetland areas have been drained that there are not many places left with this type of environment. There used to be meadows beside most rivers in Great Britain. These mostly flooded in winter, though summer downpours could also make them flood. Farmers did not plow up the meadows, so natural grasses and wildflowers were able to grow there. The meadows were kept fertile by silt from flooding and manure from cattle.

Some of the natural vegetation in these meadows is now very rare. The wildlife that use these areas is also under threat. An area used by a species of animal is called its **habitat**. Water birds such as mallard and teal use wetlands in winter. In spring, wading birds such as snipe use their pointed beaks to dig out worms and insects from the rich mud. As more land is protected from flooding and more wetland areas are drained, there is a real danger that the habitats of these species will be destroyed.

In 1990, the Dutch government announced a plan to help create new areas of wetlands. This meant flooding land that farmers had reclaimed 100 years ago. This will give a greater variety of species to the country. It may also help to control flooding by giving water somewhere useful to go.

Photo Notes
- The Somerset Levels in southwest England.
- A wetland area that is the habitat for a rich variety of wildlife.
- A large part of this area has been drained for farming, though some parts have now been preserved as conservation areas.

Conserving the Everglades

Many areas of wetlands are now being **conserved** so that their unique plant and wildlife is not lost forever. The Everglades is one of the best known wetlands in the United States. This is an area in Florida that is mostly under less than 7 feet of both freshwater and seawater. There are small islands called hammocks and winding creeks called bayous. This gives a rich variety of wildlife and vegetation.

This is one of the few places brown bears, cougars, and alligators can live in the United States without causing problems to people. They need space to live and hunt. They also need protection from hunters who want their skins. The alligator is an **endangered species**. The Everglades is home for herons, snowy egrets, and great ibis. They need to be undisturbed. All the plants and animals in the Everglades depend on each other to survive. They are part of a **food chain** that could easily be broken.

In 1947, part of the Everglades was made a **national park**. Before that, it was slowly

being polluted, drained, and reclaimed for farming and housing. Tourists now visit Everglades National Park in small numbers. But water pollution is still a problem, and commercial pressures still exist.

Many people now realize that the few remaining wetland areas need to be left for wildlife and natural vegetation. Without protection, species will become extinct and the world will be poorer without them.

Photo Notes

- The Everglades wetlands in Florida.
- An area that is being threatened by water pollution and building.
- Rare plants and wildlife are now preserved in Everglades National Park.

Eroding the Coast

POWERFUL waves crash against the land along the coastlines. There are few parts of the landscape that can change faster. Miles of land can wear away in a few hours. Protecting people against these forces is never easy.

Cliff Collapse

One news story in 1993 showed how quickly a coastline can change. The Holbeck Hall Hotel had stood on the cliffs at Scarborough on the east coast of England since 1883. For a hundred years, the clear sea views attracted visitors to stay there. Then without warning, cracks began to appear and the ground started to collapse. Guests looked on as a large part of the hotel and its grounds slid down the cliff and into the sea. Erosion had worn back the cliff until it was no longer stable. The collapse just had to come.

Coastlines are eroded every day by waves, wind, and rain. Waves pound the cliffs like battering rams. Soft, loose rocks such as clays are worn back quite quickly. Pieces break off and fall to the bottom. These are soon picked up by the waves and taken away. This allows the waves to get at the bottom of the cliff again. More is worn away until the material above collapses again.

Rainwater soaks into soft rock and makes it heavier. It also makes it easier for the rocks to slide. After a period of heavy rain, parts of a cliff can collapse under its own weight. It is very hard to stop this from happening. People who buy a house with a sea view need to take great care.

Photo Notes

- The Holbeck Hall Hotel in Scarborough, England, collapsed after erosion by the sea made the cliff unstable.
- Rain soaked into the loose clay and caused a landslide.

Lowlands at Risk

Material that is carried away from a cliff is washed along the coast and then dropped. This is how a beach is made. Sand and pebbles are washed up on the beach at the angle of the incoming waves. As the wave goes back again, they are pulled straight down the beach. This gives a zigzag movement that makes the material move along the coast. This movement is called **longshore drift**.

Without a beach, the land behind it is directly exposed to the power of the waves. This is why there always needs to be a supply of sand and pebbles washed along the coast.

Some stretches of coastline are protected by lines of sand dunes. These can grow behind a wide, sandy beach. The wind dries out the sand when the tide goes out. Dry sand is then blown onshore where it piles up as sand dunes. The dunes are held in place by grasses that have long, deep roots. The grasses help to trap more sand as it blows from the beach.

Too many people heading for the beach can trample the grasses and destroy them. People can also wear down a track that the wind blows through. This can be the start of a **blow out**, which blows a hollow through the dune. This can allow the sea to come through and flood the land behind it.

A large part of Somerset in southwest England is protected from the sea by a beach and low sand dunes. Without them, the sea could flood inland over a lowland area called the Somerset Levels. Hundreds of villages and farms would be ruined if this ever happened.

DID YOU KNOW?

Erosion can be both helpful and harmful. While it may threaten communities along coastlines, it has produced some of the world's most breathtakingly beautiful geological formations. The Grand Canyon was created over millions of years by erosion from the Colorado River.

Tides and Weather

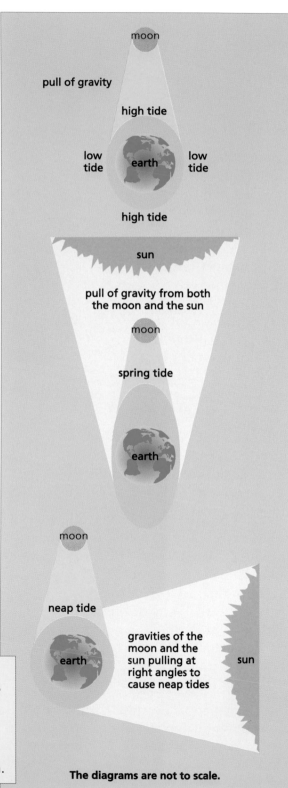

THE risk of a flood by the sea is greatest when the waves come furthest up the beach and when they are strongest. High tides and windy weather blowing onshore give these conditions. High-tide times can be worked out well in advance. It is not so easy to predict the weather. There is a small chance in any one year that a high tide and strong onshore winds will come at the same time. Unfortunately this does sometimes happen with dreadful results.

High and Low Tide

The tide comes in then goes out once every 12 hours and 20 minutes. There is a high tide when the moon pulls the water toward it by its **gravity**. This is the force that a large object has to pull another object toward itself. On the sides of the earth away from the moon, the oceans are pulled thinner, making the tide go out. This leaves a high tide on the opposite side of the earth to the moon. So the side facing the moon and the side directly opposite it both have high tides and then low tides at the same time.

The highest tides occur when the sun and the moon are in a direct line with the earth. Gravity from both of them together raises the sea level by an extra amount. These special high tides are called **spring tides**. The opposite to a spring tide is a **neap tide**, when the tide is at its lowest.

Photo Notes

- Tides are caused by the pull of gravity from the moon and the sun.
- There are high tides on opposite sides of the earth at the same time.
- The highest tides are when the sun and the moon are both pulling from the same direction.

Diagram labels:

moon

pull of gravity

high tide

low tide — earth — low tide

high tide

sun

pull of gravity from both the moon and the sun

moon

spring tide

earth

moon

neap tide

earth

gravities of the moon and the sun pulling at right angles to cause neap tides

sun

The diagrams are not to scale.

Wind and Waves

The wind causes most ocean waves. The height of waves depends on the speed of the wind, how long it blows, and the distance it blows over the ocean. So the faster the wind, the longer it blows, and the greater its distance, the bigger the waves. As the wind blows out to sea, waves grow to their greatest height and then break. After the wind stops, the waves continue to move over the ocean surface and can travel great distances from where they were formed. This distance is called the **fetch**.

As waves move toward the shore, the water becomes shallow. This is when the wave crest falls over and forms **breakers**. Waves become smaller and less powerful as they move further up the beach. By the time the waves have stopped moving forward, most of their power to erode has gone.

Waves are at their most powerful when the wind is blowing them directly onto a coastline where the water is deep. The full force of the waves then hits the shore and great damage can be done.

There is no link between the weather and the time when there are high tides. But sometimes the two act together by chance. In 1953, this combination brought chaos to the coastlines of both Great Britain and the Netherlands.

DID YOU KNOW?

The greatest difference between high and low tide is in the Bay of Fundy in Canada. The average tide difference is 53.2 feet.

Low-lying areas were battered by storm-force winds that broke through the **sea walls**. Over 300 people were drowned. In the Netherlands, the death toll was 1,800. People living on islands where land was below sea level stood no chance. There was no high ground to go to and no way to escape.

Both of these areas have built better defenses since then. There is still the danger that the sea and the wind will combine to win again. An added problem is that the defenses will grow older and will need to be kept in good repair.

Photo Notes
- Strong winds blow waves onto a breakwater.
- There is deep water before the breakwater so the full force of the waves can come in.
- The bottom part of the breakwater absorbs some of the waves' forces.

Defending the Coast

Photo Notes
- A high shingle beach counters the force of the waves.
- A low concrete sea wall and an embankment protect the land behind.
- The flat land has been reclaimed from marshes for farming.
- Cracks in the sea wall must be kept filled to keep the sea from making them wider.

THERE are places that need to be protected from being flooded or washed away by the sea. Seaside resorts and ports, roads, railroads, and farmland are all at risk of being washed away or flooded. The cost of defending the coast is very high. The cost of repairing the damage that the sea can do may be even higher.

Saving the Beach

A beach stops the full force of the waves from reaching the land behind it. This is why it is so important to make sure that sand and pebbles are kept on the beach. Longshore drift moves material along the coast. This can be slowed down if barriers are built down the beach. These barriers are called **groins**. Wood, metal, or concrete groins are a common sight at seaside resorts. People need a beach to relax on, and the town needs a beach to defend it from the sea.

People in Withernsea on the east coast of England are trying to save their town from the sea. Their beach is being washed away, and they fear that the town will be next to go. To solve the problem, large stones have been dumped between wooden groins. They hope that this will help delay the time when the sea will break through.

Concrete and stone sea walls are also used to protect a coast. There are different types. Some have straight, vertical walls. Others are built at an angle. A sea wall with a curved top makes one wave fall back on the next incoming wave so that its power is reduced. They are also built in steps to break up the force of the waves. Even the strongest stone and concrete walls are broken by waves. Building them is expensive, but they last a long time if they are repaired when they are damaged.

Using Nature

Sand dunes can be protected by keeping people off them and providing footpaths built from wooden planks or plastic mats. This keeps the footpath from being worn down into a gap that the wind could blow through and make wider and deeper.

Marram grass grows well on sand dunes if it is not trampled. Fencing off the dunes protects it, and more grass can be planted to replace what has been destroyed.

Trees planted on the dunes stop them from being blown or washed away. Conifers are best, as they grow quickly and can survive in dry, sandy conditions. Using nature may be the best and cheapest way to protect the dunes and the land behind them.

East Anglia on England's east coast is badly in need of better sea defenses. The coastline has every kind of problem. The rock is very soft, and the land is low-lying and exposed to strong winds from the North Sea. The sea level is slowly rising, and the land is slowly sinking. There are already 1,000

miles of sea walls and other defenses but even this might not be enough. About 750,000 people in the area live below the level of the high tide. They are at risk of coastal flooding if the sea defenses break.

Salt marshes could keep the force of the waves away from the land. Previously these were reclaimed from the sea and used as farmland. Now, the natural vegetation in salt marshes is left to take the force of the waves before they reach the shore. This will also help conserve habitats for birds and other wildlife. Sometimes, living with nature is better than trying to fight it.

Photo Notes
- The beach and sand dunes on the Bay of Biscay in France.
- The beach is popular with tourists, but the sand dunes have to be protected.
- Large areas of the dunes are fenced off, and new marram grass has been planted.

The Dutch Fight Back

THE Dutch people must know more about floods and how to control them than anyone else. Almost half the people live below sea level and millions more live near to some of Europe's largest rivers. Keeping the sea out and the rivers in has been a battle that the Dutch have been fighting for centuries.

Keeping the Sea Out

The Rhine, Mass, and Scheldt rivers all flow out to the North Sea in the southern part of the Netherlands. Mud from the rivers has made islands in this delta area. Over the years, people have built farms on the islands. **Dikes** have been built to keep the sea out.

In 1953, there was a flood disaster when strong winds and a high tide broke through the dikes. About 1,800 people drowned, and there was widespread damage. Thousands of farm animals also drowned.

To make sure this would never happen again, the Dutch have built dams across the estuaries. This work has now been finished. The dams link the ends of the islands nearest to the sea. This will make the islands safe for as long as the dams are high enough and strong enough to beat the power of the sea.

Photo Notes
- A dam that stops the sea from coming in among the islands of the delta area.
- Dams were built to link the seaward ends of all the islands in the delta after the 1953 flood disaster.
- Ships can pass through a lock in this dam.

Rivers and Coast

Forty years after the disaster in the delta area, the Dutch are still trying to control their rivers and coastline. The Rhine River splits up into the Lek and Waal rivers as it enters the Netherlands. They then flow over flat valley land to the North Sea. Dikes along the riverbanks give people some protection, but severe floods in 1993 were another reminder that the problem has not been solved. Thousands had to leave their homes as the rivers flooded once more.

River floods can come in the Netherlands at different times of the year. Melting snow and ice flows down the rivers from the Alps during spring and early summer. The meltwater flows into the Rhine River and quickly raises its level. Winter storms can also cause flooding when too much rain flows into the tributaries that feed into the larger rivers. The Dutch people can see the floods coming for at least two days as the Rhine flows through Germany. People are alerted, so their lives are not usually put at risk.

Dikes can be built higher to stop the flooding, but not everyone agrees that this is the right answer. A dike is shaped like a triangle when seen from the side. For every 1 foot the dike is built higher, the base of the dike has to be built several more feet wider. As the dikes are built

Photo Notes
- Flat **polderland** below sea and river level that has to be protected from flooding.
- Dams and dikes need to be high enough to keep floodwater out.
- If the land does flood, the water would have to be pumped back up over the dikes.

wider, homes and whole villages may need to be torn down. One engineer has said the river defenses could look like a fifteen-lane expressway that stretches for 370 miles. There is now a plan to make some parts of the dikes higher by the year 2004.

Sand dunes protect the western coast of the Netherlands against the North Sea. These are sometimes 165 feet high, but they are made of sand and grasses. The sea and the wind can wash and blow them away. Dikes have been built in places where there is a break in the line of dunes. The dunes and dikes are all that stops the North Sea from rolling in over the Dutch countryside. This is why it is so important to make sure that they are well maintained.

DID YOU KNOW?

Two-fifths of the Netherlands was covered by the sea before the Dutch pumped out water to create fertile farmland.

Saving Cities

LONDON and Venice are two cities with something in common. They are both sinking. As they sink, the risk of flooding by the sea becomes greater. Each city has to find its own answer to this problem.

London's Flood Barrier

A **flood barrier** was completed across the Thames River in 1983. This was needed to stop the central part of London from being flooded. Part of the problem is that the city is built on an area of clays. The weight of the city is making it sink. The whole of southeast England is also slowly sinking.

London's position causes another problem. The Thames flows through London then out to the North Sea through the Thames estuary. The estuary acts as a giant funnel to the incoming tide. Water is forced higher as it moves up the estuary. Docks have been built along the estuary banks. This stops the high tide from flooding along the estuary. Instead, the water moves further upstream toward the center of London.

The greatest risk of flood is when there are strong north winds and a low-pressure area over the North Sea. There is less weight of air pressing down on the sea under a low-pressure area. This lets the sea rise. North winds blow the sea toward London, and the water builds up in the Thames estuary. This is called a **storm surge**.

The flood barrier is designed to hold back the water when a high tide and a storm surge come together. The barrier should make London safe for some years to come.

Photo Notes
- The Thames flood barrier in London.
- Steel shutters rotate to make a wall to hold back the tidewater.
- The barrier has been raised many times; so far, it has always protected the city.

Saving Venice

Venice is one of the world's most unusual cities. It was started in the fifth century in an area of lagoons in the Adriatic Sea. At first, houses were built on wooden posts that were sunk vertically into the mud. Over the years, stone has replaced the wood to form some of the finest buildings in Europe. The Doge's Palace and St. Mark's Cathedral are two of the best known of these. Each time a house was rebuilt, new foundations were built on top of the old foundations. This has made the houses strong but very heavy.

There have always been floods in Venice, but they are getting worse. The weight of the stone buildings is slowly making the city sink into the mud by about one quarter of an inch each year.

People have made the problem worse by taking water out of the rocks beneath the mud. The water is being used by new factories that have been built on the mainland near Venice.

There is a small difference between the high and low tides in the Mediterranean. At the moment, flooding is mainly caused when there is a high tide at the same time that strong winds blow south from the mountains. The waves and high tide are sometimes enough to raise the sea level above the level of the pavement. This has flooded buildings and caused great damage to the city's art treasures. Floods in 1966 caused great damage that has taken years to restore.

One solution is to build better sea walls around the lagoon so that waves cannot get to the city. Another is to pump water back into the rocks so that the city stops sinking. Other ways may be found to stop the buildings from sinking, but none is cheap or easy. A rise in the sea level because of **global warming** will make the problem worse. There is little time left to make sure that something is done.

After the Flood

PEOPLE die and are injured during floods. Their belongings are washed away and ruined. For the survivors, many of the problems are only just starting. The way that people can recover depends on where they live. In rich countries, money can be found to help. In poorer countries, people have to help themselves.

Starting Again

Floods in rich countries do not usually kill or injure many people. Most are able to survive, though they often lose much of what they own. The cost of the damage can be enormous, because people own so much. Some people insure their property so that it can be replaced if it is lost or damaged. They are left with nothing if they have no savings or if they are not insured against floods.

In 1990, Towyn in north Wales was flooded when the sea broke through the defenses. About 6,400 acres were flooded under 6 feet of seawater. Almost 3,000 homes and other buildings were flooded. Towyn is a popular area for vacations.

Water flooded through the trailer parks, and many of them were completely destroyed.

Floods mean that people have to move out of their homes. In 1993, more sea floods in north Wales made another 2,000 homes unfit to live in. The whole town of Llandudno had to be evacuated. People had to have emergency accommodations organized by the government, which used government buildings for people who could not stay with friends or relatives.

In Towyn, only one in every three people was insured against the loss. A disaster fund was set up and raised about $1.5 million. The government used money from taxes to help people replace some of what was lost.

A new sea wall has now been built, this time higher and stronger than before.

Photo Notes
- People return to their homes in Towyn after the floods have gone down.
- Carpets, furniture, and other belongings are all ruined by the muddy saltwater.
- Not everyone was insured for the losses.

From Bad to Worse

Floods that affect people in poor countries bring enormous problems to the survivors. Many families will have lost a relative. A big flood is reported in newspapers and on television all over the world. Disaster appeals are organized, and people send money to help. The governments in poor countries rarely have enough money to help the victims or to build better flood defenses.

Floods can wash away houses that have poor foundations and are made of wood and scrap materials. People lose everything they own and cannot repair the damage. In 1991, the Wardha River in India burst its banks. About 500 people were killed and 10,000 were made homeless.

Emergency centers where people live in tents are sometimes set up. People have to live here until they are able to move back and rebuild their homes.

Rescue work is often made difficult because

Photo Notes
- An emergency camp in the Philippines after flash floods destroyed thousands of homes.
- Disease from dirty water and poor sanitation causes problems in these camps.

roads and bridges are washed away and there is not enough rescue equipment. Diseases such as cholera often come after a flood. Water supplies are disrupted and become polluted with sewage. Cholera spreads quickly where people are crowded together in poor living conditions.

In country areas, floods destroy crops and animals that people need for food. Crops cannot be replaced until new seeds are bought and the crops have time to grow. They cannot be planted until animals are replaced to plow the land.

Conditions such as these make real human disasters. Emergency aid is not able to solve problems on this kind of scale. It would be helpful for the future if more money could be spent to stop the floods from happening so often and with such force.

Rising Seas

DEFENSES against flooding must be able to survive the worst kind of problems that might happen. There is no point in building defenses that are too low or too weak. There is also no point in building defenses that are much higher or stronger than is needed. This is why information about the flow of rivers, the height of tides, and the weather is so important. A problem is that defenses need to last for a very long time. Within that time, the weather and the sea level might change in ways that are not properly predicted.

The Greenhouse Effect

Some scientists say there is evidence that the temperature in the atmosphere is becoming warmer. This effect is called global warming. The scientists say that this is being caused by an increase in the amount of carbon dioxide and other gases in the air.

These gases let heat from the sun come through the atmosphere, but they trap it as it reflects back to space. This is called the **greenhouse effect**.

It is hard to be certain about what might happen next. If the temperature rises, the amount of water in the seas and oceans will grow. More water will be added to the oceans as snow and glaciers melt. The greenhouse effect could raise the level of the sea by several feet within the next 50 to 100 years. Places that are already at risk could be flooded if sea walls and other defenses are not built high enough.

Photo Notes
- The greenhouse effect, which might cause global warming.
- Air that is heated becomes trapped in the atmosphere by carbon dioxide and other "greenhouse" gases.

Photo Notes

- The Maldive Islands in the Indian Ocean.
- There are almost 1,100 small coral islands in this part of the Indian Ocean.
- People live on just 200 of these islands.
- Rising sea levels are threatening the islands.

People at Risk

A rise in the world sea level could put 500 million people at risk of being flooded. Most of these people live in the world's largest cities. These cities are in every continent. Tokyo, London, New Orleans, Rio de Janeiro, and Alexandria are some of the cities that could be affected first. It is hard to imagine that they could be abandoned and left to the sea. The cost of moving everybody and rebuilding these cities would be even greater than the cost of building sea defenses to protect them.

There could also be problems on the low coral islands in the Pacific and Indian oceans. A higher sea level could flood completely over many of them. It is impossible to build sea defenses around every island. This would be too expensive, and there is no guarantee that the defenses would work. There may be no other choice except to abandon them.

The greenhouse effect may bring other changes that could cause problems. If the sea and air become warmer, there could be more hurricanes and other extremes of weather. There could be more rain from thunderstorms, so the rivers would be more likely to flood. More hurricanes and a higher sea level would spell disaster for people who live near the coast in tropical areas.

Flood defenses need to be built to last, but it is hard to know exactly what conditions will be like in the future.

DID YOU KNOW?

In January 1993, it was decided that five of the 200 inhabited Maldive Islands in the Indian Ocean were no longer safe. The islands are being worn away by slowly rising seawater. The people are to be evacuated to other islands.

Glossary

alluvial *see* alluvium

alluvium material carried by a river and deposited in a valley flood plain

beach sand and other material on the foreshore between land and sea

blow out a hollow in a sand dune blown out by the wind

breakers wave crests that fall over as waves move forward

channel the bed and sides of a river

cloudburst a sudden downpour of rain

condense cool and change from a gas to a liquid

conserve manage so as to protect

cumulonimbus a large type of rain cloud

deforestation large scale clearance of trees

deposition material that is dropped

dike an embankment to protect land against flooding

discharge the amount of water flowing in a river

drainage basin the area that is drained by a river system

endangered species plants or animals that are at risk of becoming extinct

estuary the mouth of a river where it widens as it enters the sea

evaporation the change from a liquid to a gas

fetch the unsheltered distance a wave travels

flash flood a sudden rise in a river level, which causes a flood

flood barrier barrier built across a river, below the normal surface level, which can be raised to stop floodwater from moving upstream

flood plain flat land in a valley bottom that is regularly flooded

food chain the food links between different animals

gabions rocks held together in wire cages, used to protect land from erosion

gas a substance that has been evaporated from a liquid

global warming the idea that the earth's atmosphere is becoming warmer

gravity the force with which one object pulls on another object

greenhouse effect the way that some gases in the atmosphere keep back heat that is being reflected back to space

groin a barrier on a beach that is designed to slow down longshore drift

habitat the environment in which a species of wildlife lives

impermeable not allowing water to sink through

infiltration water that sinks down through soil and rock

land reclamation drain water from a lake or the sea and make it dry land

levees natural or artificial embankments along a river bank

longshore drift the movement of material along a coast

manage control what happens by planning

marram grass a type of grass with long roots, often found in sand dunes

meanders the winding course of a river

monsoon a season where there is a change in wind direction, though the rainy season is commonly called the monsoon

mouth where a river enters the sea

national park an area in which the landscape, wildlife, and natural vegetation are conserved

navigable suitable for boats

neap tide a tide that is lower than the average

permeable allows water to sink through

polderland land below sea level that has been reclaimed

pores small spaces between grains in a rock or between particles of soil

regime the annual pattern of a river's flow

reservoir an artificial lake where water is stored

river system the network of streams and rivers that are linked in a drainage basin

salt marsh an area of marsh that is covered by the sea at high tide

sand dunes low hills of sand that pile up behind a beach

sea level the level down to which rivers flow when they enter the sea

sea wall a concrete or stone wall built to defend a coast against erosion

silt fine particles of mud that are carried in a river

solid a hard substance that has a definite shape

source the place where a river rises

spring a place where groundwater flows out of a rock

spring tide the highest tide levels, which occur when the gravity of the moon and sun acts from the same direction

storm surge a special high tide, which occur when the sea level rises during a depression

stream a small river

surface run-off rainwater that flows off the surface to a river

tide the daily rise and fall of the sea level

transpiration evaporation of water from vegetation

tributary a small river that joins a larger river

water cycle the movement of water from sea to land, then back to sea

water table the level of water between saturated and unsaturated layers of rock

water vapor water in the form of a gas

waterlogged soil or rock in which all the pore spaces are filled with water so that no more can sink through

watershed the dividing line between two drainage basins

wetland land that is regularly covered by shallow water

Index

Adriatic Sea 41
Alexandria 45
Algeria 13
alluvium 15, 17, 25
Alps 10, 12, 19, 39
Amazon 11
Arkansas 26
Asia 17, 20, 22
Atlantic Ocean 11, 35
atmosphere 6, 7, 45

Bangladesh 16, 23, 27, 29
bayous 15, 31
beach 5, 33, 34, 35, 36
Bengal, Bay of 23
Benue 11
Berkshire 19
Bible 5
Biscay, Bay of 37
blow out 33
Brahmaputra 16, 22, 23
breakwater 35

Camargue 15
Cameroon 11
Canada 35
channels 9, 10, 12, 13, 14, 15, 20, 21, 25, 28, 29
Chichester 13
China 5, 15, 17, 29
China's sorrow 5
cholera 43
clay 9, 32, 33, 40
cliff 32
climate 12
cloudburst 13
clouds 6, 7, 13, 45
coastline 5, 7, 32, 33, 36, 37, 39
Cologne 12
conifers 37
conservation 20, 31, 37
coral islands 45
Costa Rica 8
cumulonimbus 13
currents (see ocean currents)

dams 28, 38
Dee 14
deforestation 20
delta 15, 23, 24, 38
deposition 5, 14
depressions 19
desert 13
Des Moines 25

Devon 18
Dhaka 16
dikes 38, 39
disaster area 26
discharge 12
downpour 8, 19, 30
drainage 21, 30
drainage basin 10, 11, 22, 23, 25, 26
dredging 29
Dutch 30, 38, 39

East Anglia 35, 37
Egypt 16
electricity 28
electricity power station 15
embankments 15, 16, 29, 36
emergency aid 43
endangered species 31
England 10, 18, 32, 33, 35, 36, 37, 40
erosion 5, 14, 32
estuary 11, 38, 40
Europe 11, 18, 19, 21, 38, 41
evaporation 6, 7, 8, 10, 11, 13, 20
Everglades 31

flash flood 13, 23, 43
flood barrier 40
flood defenses 4, 5, 18, 21, 24, 25, 27
flood plain 14, 15, 17
floodwater 4, 16, 27
Florida 31
France 10, 15, 19, 21
Fundy, Bay of 35

gabions 29
Ganges 16, 22, 23
Germany 12, 21, 39
glaciers 6, 7, 10, 12, 45
global warming 41, 45
gravity 34
Great Britain 13, 19, 30, 35
greenhouse effect 45
greenhouse gases 44
groins 36
Guinea, Gulf of 11
gulleys 10, 20

habitat 30, 37
hammocks 31
high tide (see tides)
Himalayas 20, 22
Holbeck Hall 32
Huang He 5, 15, 29
Hull 33
hurricanes 45
hydrogen 6

ice 12, 39
icebergs 6
ice sheets 7
India 12, 16, 17, 22, 23, 43
Indian Ocean 45
Indus 22
infiltration 9
Iowa 26, 27
irrigation 17
Italy 19

landslides 22
Lavant 13
Lek 39
levees 15, 25, 26, 27, 29
limestone 9
Llandudno 19, 42
locks 28
London 40, 45
longshore drift 33, 36

Maldive Islands 45
management 21, 29
marram grass 37
marshes 9, 36
Mass 38
meanders 14, 24, 25, 29
Mediterranean Sea 41
Memphis 25
Mexico, Gulf of 24
Minnesota 24, 26
Mississippi 15, 24, 25, 26, 27, 29
Missouri 24
monsoon 12, 22, 23
mountains 7
mouth 11, 24
mud 9, 13, 15, 17, 18, 24, 25, 28, 38, 41, 42

national park 31
natural defenses (see flood defenses)
nature reserves 17
navigation 25, 28

neap tides 34
Nepal 20
Netherlands 12, 35, 39
New Orleans 24, 45
Niger 11
Nile 11
North Sea 37, 38, 40
Norway 7

ocean currents 6
Ohio 13, 26
Oxford 16
oxygen 6

Pacific Ocean 45
Paris 4
pebbles 33, 36
Perth 18
Philippines 22, 23, 43
polderland 39
pollution 31, 43
pores 9
Porthcawl 35

radar 19
rain 4, 6, 7, 8, 13, 20, 32, 45
rainbow 5
rainstorm 8, 21, 39
reclamation 5, 30, 31, 36
reservoirs 28
Rhine 12, 38, 39
Rhône 10, 15
river banks 5, 12, 13, 18, 19, 21, 25, 29, 39
river system 11
run-off 9, 13, 20

salt marshes 37
Salt River 28
sand 5, 17, 28, 33, 36, 39
sand dunes 5, 33, 37, 39
sandstone 9
Scarborough 32, 33, 34
Scheldt 38
Scotland 18
sea defenses 37, 45
sea floods 5, 23
sea level 7
seaside resorts 36
sea walls 35, 36, 37, 42
Severn 11, 15
sewage 43

Shadyside 13
shantytowns 22
shingle 5
silt 15, 17, 30
snow 4, 6, 7, 9, 12, 18, 39, 45
Somerset Levels 30
Spain 19
spring tides 34
St. Louis 24, 25, 27
St. Mark's, Venice 41
storm force 35
storm surge 40
streams 4, 7, 10, 12, 22
Switzerland 12, 19

Tay 18
Tennessee 24, 26
Thames 10, 40
thunder clouds 13, 45
thunderstorms 19
tides 5, 33, 34, 35, 38, 40, 41, 44
Towyn 42
transpiration 8
tributary 11, 24, 27
tropical rain forest 8, 20
typhoons 23

United States 9, 24, 31

valleys 14, 17, 19, 24, 26, 27
vegetation 8, 22
Venice 19, 40, 41

Waal 39
Wales 19, 35, 42
Wardha 43
water cycle 6, 7
waterlogging 19, 21, 26
watershed 10
water table 9
water vapor 6, 13
wetlands 15, 27, 30, 31
wind 6, 32, 35, 40
Withernsea 36

Floods mentioned in this book are printed in bold.

48